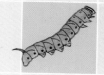

Where's God?

BY KAREN KING

ILLUSTRATED BY
JANE COPE

VICTOR BOOKS
A DIVISION OF SCRIPTURE PRESS PUBLICATIONS INC.
USA CANADA ENGLAND

"Goodnight, Katy. God bless,"
said Mom as she tucked Katy into bed.
"You always say that!" Katy told her.
"*Who* is God?"
"God is the one who made the world,"
said Mom.
"He made you, me, and everything else!
Now, goodnight. Sleep tight."

But Katy couldn't sleep.
She kept thinking about God.
What did He look like?
Where was He?
Was God in the sky?
She ran over to the window to look.

The next morning Katy got up very early.
She wanted to look for God.
First she searched all around the house,
just in case He was hiding.

Later, Mom and Katy went for a walk.
Katy wondered if she would find God
while they were out.
Perhaps He was by the stream.

Then they went to the beach.
Katy ran along the sand, looking for God.

Soon it was time to go home.
But Katy still hadn't found God.
"Where are you, God?" she called.
"What are you looking for, Katy?"
asked Mom.
"I'm trying to find God," Katy said.

"Oh, Katy!" smiled Mom.
"God is everywhere! You can't *see* Him.
But you can see something of what He's like
in everything He has made."
Katy thought about all the things she had seen...
and she smiled.

Lift the flap to see some of the things God has made.
Can you play the game?

1 2 3 4 5 6 7 8 9 10 Printing /Year 96 95

Published in the United States by Victor Books/
SP Publications, Inc., Wheaton, Illinois.
Printed in Singapore.

ISBN: 1-56476-467-2